EVERYTHING YOU WANT TO KNOW ABOUT RECIPES AND RESTAURANTS AND MUCH MORE

This Book Is Designed For Celiac Sprue People Looking For Gluten Free Ideas

Erik and Jennifer Spersrud

authorHOUSE®

AuthorHouse™
1663 Liberty Drive, Suite 200
Bloomington, IN 47403
www.authorhouse.com
Phone: 1-800-839-8640

First published by AuthorHouse 11/8/2007

ISBN: 978-1-4343-4352-9 (sc)

Printed in the United States of America
Bloomington, Indiana

This book is printed on acid-free paper.

INTRODUCTION

Hi, my name is Jennifer. I am a thirty-nine-year-old mom of two children, nineteen and eight years old, with a wonderful husband. He has been at my side, struggling with my disease, for ten years. I first noticed something wasn't right at twelve years old. At the time my family and I lived in Boston. My mom took me to the doctor for stomach problems. They did a GI series. And I was put on Maalox. Then the symptoms started. I was running to the bathroom during mealtime because of diarrhea. As I got older, around 1993 I was starting to have sharp pains in my neck and back. Then they did another scope down my throat and found acid reflex. I was put on medicine for that. But I still was getting sick. Years went by with me having pains in my neck and back and still having diarrhea.

I did not know yet I had celiac sprue disease. Things got really bad. When I was pregnant with my second child, I was getting sick every day. I would stay in bed for days at a time. My life was very unhappy. I moved to Indiana in 2004. And my health was still awful. I didn't know about celiac sprue disease yet. One day in August 2004, I was having chest pains. So I went to my family doctor for a checkup. The next day my blood work came back. And the doctor called my husband, looking for me. The doctor said, "Take your wife to the hospital ASAP." My husband took me to the hospital. I was admitted to ICU right away. My hemoglobin count dropped to a level four. They said there was not enough blood going to my heart.

I was bleeding internally. I lost three pints of blood. A blood transfusion was done ASAP. Then all the testing started. I was there for six days. It was very hard on me and my family. Another scope was performed. And a biopsy was done. Tissue samples showed that I had celiac sprue disease. All these years I was poisoning myself with gluten. Gluten was poisoning my body.

If you have had theses symptoms at least once a week during the past three months, go to your doctor and get a blood test and diagnosis. Here are some of the symptoms: bloating, stomach cramping, diarrhea, constipation, joint pain, numbness or tingling in your arms and legs, itching skin lesions, constant unexplained fatigue, frequent headaches or migraines. I want you to know that there is light at the end of the tunnel. Gluten is wheat flour and barley and oats. You are probably thinking, what I can eat? Well that's why my husband and I put this book together. The book tells you about food to buy, stores to shop at, and restaurants to eat at. Now that I know what was causing my condition, I am doing much better after changing my eating habits.

I am really enjoying life. And you can too. In 2008, we will have gluten-free labels on all food products. Celiac sprue disease is an autoimmune disorder that affects one in every one hundred people. Ninety-seven percent of the population doesn't know they have it and continue to suffer with the symptoms. Change your life, like I did, and be happy. Enjoy this book.

Starting a gluten-free (GF) diet is pretty easy. The GF diet is a lifelong commitment.

1. **Start Simply – Keep a Diary**
Start with unprocessed foods such as fresh fruits, vegetables, meat, rice, and potatoes. These are things that don't need gluten-free labels. Use olive oil, salt, pepper, and lemon juice, for seasoning. This may be a bit boring but can help the intestines heal rapidly. Some people diagnosed

with celiac disease find that foods that contain lactose or have a high fat content can be difficult to digest at first, but they later may be well tolerated as the intestines begin to repair themselves. Keep a record of the foods eaten and how they make you feel. Add new foods as they are tolerated. Keep track of the gluten-free specialty products and recipes you try, writing down which you did not.

2. Find Support Group

Support groups are a very good resource for leaning about celiac disease and the gluten-free diet. Consider becoming a member of the Gluten Intolerance Group of North American, a national support organization working with others to improve the lives of people with celiac and other Gluten-intolerance diseases. Look them up on the Web.

3. Learn about Your Diet

Read everything you can on celiac disease and gluten-free items. If possible, make an appointment to visit a registered dietician. A lot of items contain gluten. Be careful about anything you put in your month. Some medications and even stamp/envelope glue may contain gluten.

4. Becoming Gluten-Free

Make your kitchen gluten-free. First replace all your plastic items, Tupperware, all plastic cooking items. They have gluten in them. Replace all non-stick pans with new ones. Make sure you only cook gluten-free items in them from now on. Your kitchen needs to be gluten-free. Get a new toaster for yourself use only gluten-free bread in it. Keep track of which foods in your home are gluten-free and which are not. Clear a special shelf or area just for gluten-free foods. Or make the whole kitchen gluten-free and have a separate shelf where other members of the household can keep their gluten-containing items. Make sure everything that you use is gluten-free; for example, shampoos, hand soaps, makeup, and hand lotions. Call the manufacture before using a product to make sure it's gluten-free.

I would recommend calling the manufacture about any items you use to make sure they don't have gluten in them. A lot of products have gluten in them but it is not on the labels. So you have to be 100 percent careful of any items you use.

5. Finding Gluten-Free Foods

Grocery stores can be a good source for corn tortillas, rice, fruits, vegetables, beans, meats, fish, poultry, milk, eggs, and other naturally gluten-free foods.

Wild Oats is one of the best grocery stores. They have everything labeled gluten-free; plus everybody is the store is very helpful. They are a big national chain located almost everywhere in the United States.

Good Earth Natural Food stores are another source to get gluten-free items.

Health food stores can be a good source for gluten-free bread, pasta, cereal, cookies, baking mixes, flours, etc.

Oriental markets can be a great source for finely ground rice flour, potato flour, and tapioca flour at a very low price.

Mail-order vendors can be good sources for hard-to-find gluten-free baked goods and mixes.

6. Take Food with You

When leaving home it is a good idea to take along some gluten-free food.

- Gluten-free energy bars, trail mix, jerky, and fruit snacks travel well in a purse, bag, or car to have on hand for emergencies.
- Gluten-free sandwiches can be packed for lunches for the office.
- Dinner leftovers make good lunches for the office.
- Have your doctor write a note if you would like to bring something to eat at ballgames and sporting events, where outside food may be restricted, especially when traveling at airports.
- Consider bringing a main dish and a side dish to potluck socials if you want to have plenty of food to eat. When attending a special event, contact the caterer or event coordinator ahead of time to ensure a proper gluten-free meal is prepared.
- When possible eat well before social gatherings so you can simply enjoy the company.

7. Eat Gluten-Free when Dining Out

- When dining at a restaurant, look for menu items that can easily be made gluten-free.
- Grilled meat, fish, and poultry; baked potatoes, and steamed vegetables are examples of dishes that often can be prepared without gluten.
- If it is your first time eating a gluten-free meal at the restaurant, you may want to speak with the chief. Also you may want to share a restaurant card with the server or chef. Restaurant cards that briefly explain the gluten-free diet are available from gluten-intolerance groups. I have also included one in this book.
- Ask your server for help in choosing a menu selection, and let your server know that your meal must be prepared gluten-free.

For example, the server needs to know that when you order a salad without croutons, it is not okay to remove the croutons from a prepared salad. The salad must be made fresh, without contacting gluten-containing ingredients.

- If your streak is being cooked on a grill that is also used for breaded items, then your selection should be prepared on a piece of aluminum foil or in a clean pan.
- Check the ingredients in any marinades and seasonings, or ask to have your meat and vegetables prepared without seasonings.
- French fries prepared in the same oil that was used for frying breaded foods, such onion rings or chicken nuggets, will not be gluten-free.
- Some restaurants have gluten-free menus. I have included a list of restaurants in this book.

While the information on this page was accurate at the time it was posted, menu ingredients can change without notice. It's is recommended you verify the information before you dine out. Remember, eating out always involves some level of risk. I have listed restaurants that cater to gluten-free customers.

ARBY'S
Meats and sauces are safe.

BASKIN-ROBBINS ICE CREAM
Baskins Robbins lists the allergen information on the flavor cards posted on the counters in front of each tub of ice cream.

BEN & JERRY'S
Gluten ingredients will be clearly listed

BOSTON MARKET

Rotisserie chicken

Rotisserie turkey breast

Sirloin without au jus

Plain grilled chicken breast

Lemon herb rotisserie chicken

Corn

Cream spinach

Butternut squash

Green beans (plain)

Mashed potatoes (no gravy)

Garlic/dill new potatoes

Broccoli with hollandaise sauce

Jumpin' Juice squares

Fruit salad

Cranberry relish

Hot cinnamon apples

BUCA DI BEPPO

Ask that the entrees not be dusted in flour.

Antipasti cold platter

Antipasti mussels marinara

1893 Salad

Mixed green salad

Chicken with lemon

Chicken marsala

Veal marsala

Chicken saltimbocca

Green beans

Garlic mashed potatoes

Escarole

Italian sausage

Spumoni with chocolate

BURGER KING

Low-carb burgers and chicken (no buns)

Low-carb angus streak burgers

Side salad

Call for GF selections.

BONE FISH

Call for GF selections. Bone Fish has a big gluten-free menu.

CARRABBA'S ITALIAN GRILL

Chicken

Steaks

Salad

Side dishes

Carrabba's has an excellent GF menu with a lot of items

CHIPOTLE

Call for GF selections.

CHILI'S

Salads

Chicken (no bun)

Steaks

Burgers (no bun)

Veggies

Chili's has a gluten-free menu and they update their GF options monthly.

CHICK-FIL-A

Some dipping sauces and dressings are gluten-free.

Chick-fil-A char-grilled chicken filet

Garden salad

Tortilla strips

Fresh fruit cup

Side salad

Cole slaw

Carrot-and-raisin salad

Chick-fil-A waffle potato fries

Hash browns

Bacon slice

Egg

Sausage patty

American cheese slice

Ice Dreams cup

Chocolate syrup

Blueberry topping

Strawberry topping

COLD STONE CREAMERY

Review GF ice-cream list.

DAIRY QUEEN

Review the GF menu list.

DENNY'S

Call for GF selections.

FLEMING'S STEAK HOUSE

Fleming's has a good selection of GF items.

Steaks

Chicken

Salads

Soups

Seafood

Veggies

Call for GF selections.

HARD ROCK CAFÉ

Potato skins

Plain chicken wings

Spring rolls

Salads

Steaks

Veggies

Mashed potatoes (no gravy)

MACARONI GRILL

Call for GF selections.

MCDONALDS

Call for GF Selections.

NOODLES & CO.

Noodles and Co. restaurants have gluten and allergy info available at the cashier's station.

OLIVE GARDEN

Let your server know you are interested in menu items especially for gluten intolerance. Your server will be happy to accommodate your request.

Salads

Steaks

Chicken

Salmon

Pork

ON THE BORDER

Beef enchilada (no sauce)

Crispy beef taco

Crispy veggie taco

Guacamole appetizer

House salad

Refried beans

Check with your server for more GF items.

OUTBACK STEAK HOUSE

Appetizers

Steak

Chicken

Salads

Ribs

Prime rib

Veggies

Salmon

Rice

Alaskan king crab

Lobster tail

Outback has a very large menu of GF items to choose from.

P.F. CHANG'S CHINA BISTRO

P.F. Chang's has a very large selection of GF items.

Soothing lettuce wraps

Shanghai cucumbers

Oriental chicken salad

Ginger chicken with broccoli

Cantonese shrimp or scallops

Philip's butter lemon chicken

Chang's spicy chicken or shrimp

Chang's lemon scallops

Moo Goo Gai Pan

Mango chicken

Rice

PANERA BREAD

Soups

Salads

Check with the cashier for the GF items.

RED ROBIN

Red Robin will do its best to customize orders to meet dietary needs.

Steak fries

Cheese

Guacamole

Black beans

Chicken drummettes

Turkey patty

Grilled salmon

Egg

Salads

Veggies

RUTH'S CHRIS STEAK HOUSE

Your server at Ruth's Chris Steak House will help with your GF selections.

Appetizers

Soups

Salads

Shrimp

Steak

Chicken

STARBUCKS

Call 800-230-LATTE for GF selections.

TCBY

TCBY has GF items. Check with the cashier for a menu.

WEBER GRILL

Check with your server for GF items.

Chicken

Steak

Veggies

Potatoes

The following restaurants listed above do cater to GF customers. Always check with your server and let them know about your medical problem. Explain your diet to them; let them know how important it is.

GENERAL LIST OF GLUTEN-FREE ITEMS

Deli meats and cheeses by Boar's Head Products
Boar's Head Products has a lot of GF products.
Call 1-800-352-6277 for complete detail of products.

All kinds of cheeses (plain, not spreads)

Milk

Eggs

Fruits

Meats (frozen or fresh; plain, no seasoning)

Butter or margarine (without wheat oil)

Brown or white rice (read labels)

Canned fruit

Vegetables (plain; fresh, canned in water, or frozen)

Wines (California wines)

Coffee (pure)

Brandy

Corn flakes (plain)

Fish (fresh, uncoated, no seasoning)

Tea (plain)

Sugar

Wine vinegar

Herbs, fresh or dried

Soy sauce (tamari-type soy sauce)

Almonds, walnuts, and other nuts (plain)

Tuna (all canned in oil or water, not sauce)

Potatoes

Cornbread (read label)

Soda

Water

GF flours
White rice flour
Tapioca flour
Potato starch

Arrowroot flour

Carob flour

Nut flour

Olive oil

Canola oil

Hydrogenated vegetable oil

Fast and easy GF products: all theses items can be found at Wild Oats Natural Marketplace and most natural food markets.

Cereal

Envirokidz

Peanut butter

Koala Crisp

Amazon

Nature's Path

Corn flakes

Barbara's

Puffins

Erewhon

Crispy brown rice w/berries

Rice twice

Crispy brown rice

Brownie Mix (Pamela's)

Gluten-Free Flours:

Bob's Red Mill

white rice flour

tapioca flour

potato starch

garbanzo bean flour

almond meal/flour

GF all-purpose baking flour

Corn-starch

Arrowhead pizza crust

Gluten-Free Pantry (baking mix)

Chocolate chip mix

Muffin mix

French bread

Piecrust

Gillian's Foods (bread crumbs)

Italian breadcrumbs

Breadcrumbs

Cajun bread crumbs

Salsa

Amy's organic salsa (mild, medium, black bean)

Green Mountain salsa (mild, medium, roasted garlic)

Refried Beans

Amy's vegetarian Organic Refried Beans

Soups

Imagine Soups Brand

Creamy Sweet Corn

Broccoli

Tomato

Sweet Potato Soup

Chicken Broth

Beef Flavored Broth

Vegetable Broth

Amy's Soups Band

Tomato

Lentil

Southwestern Vegetable

Corn Chowder

Chunky Vegetable

Potato Leek

Chili with Vegetable

Split Pea

Fantastic Foods Hearty Soup Cups

Cha-Cha Chili

Split Pea Soup

Creamy Potato

Onion

Onion Mushroom

Garlic Herb

Tuna

Wild Oats Brand

Solid white

Albacore tuna

Mayonnaise
Nasoya Nayonaise

Canola mayonnaise

Ketchup/Mustard
Wild Oats Brand

Organic ketchup

Organic mustard, yellow

Organic mustard, Dijon

Organic mustard, stone ground

Bone Suckin' Sauce
Barbeque

Mustard

Annie's
Yellow mustard

Ketchup

Marinades
Wild Oats Brand

Wasabi

Smokey Campfire

Madvascurry

Soy Sauce
Tamari soy sauce

Rice
Success Rice

Lundberg's Rice Xpress, all flavors

Salad Dressings

Annie's Naturals Brand

Raspberry Vinaigrette

Cowgirl Ranch

Balsamic Vinaigrette

Caesar

French

Honey Mustard

Roasted Red Pepper

Tuscany Italian

Drew's All Natural Brand

Garlic Italian

Roasted Garlic Peppercorn

Rosemary Balsamic

Nasoya Brand

Garden Herb

Creamy Dill

Creamy Italian

Thousand Island

Seeds Of Change Brand

Roasted Red Pepper

Greek Feta

Italian Herb

Sweet Dijon

Roasted Garlic Vinaigrette

Pizza Sauce
Eden Organic Pizza Sauce

Pasta Sauce
Amy's Sauce Brand

Family Marinara Pasta Sauce

Garlic Mushroom Pasta Sauce

Wild Mushroom Pasta Sauce

Puttanesca Pasta Sauce

Tomato Basil Pasta Sauce

Pomodoro Pasta Sauce

Walnut Acres Sauce Brand

Tomato Basil

Zesty Basil

Roasted Garlic

Marinara Herbs

Portabello Marinara

Wild Oats Sauce Band

Tomato Basil

Red Wine Marinara

Vodka Cream

Parmesan

Roasted Garlic

Cookies
Pamela's Brand

Peanut Butter

Chocolate Chip Walnut

Pecan Short Bread

Chunky Chocolate Chip

Peanut Butter Chocolate

Spicy Ginger

Espresso Chocolate Chunk

Dark Chocolate Chunk

Butter Shortbread

Lemon Shortbread

Ginger Cookies

Popcorn
Newman's Own

Tortilla Chips
Green Mountain Gringo Tortilla Chips

Wild Oats White Corn Tortilla Chips

Kettle Cooked Potato Chips
Wild Oats Brand

Jalapeno

Salt Vinegar

Honey BBQ

Cheddar

Salted Classic

Original

Barbara's Bakery
Cheese Puff Bakes, original

Cheese Puff Bakes, white cheddar

Cheese Puff, original

Cheese Puff, jalapeno

Ripple Potato Chips

Mr. Krispers Chips

Barbecue

Sea Salt & Pepper

Sour Cream & Onion

Pizza Dough

Gillian's Pizza Dough

Pizza

Amy's Cheese Pizza Rice Crust

Pie Crust

Gillian's Pie Crust

Breads

Kinnikinnick Brands (donuts, breads, buns, cookies, mixes, snacks)

877-503-4466

Food For Life Breads (Gluten-Free)

Ice Cream

Haagen Dazs Brand

Vanilla

Haagen Dazs Ice Cream Bars Brand

Chocolate & Dark Bars

Vanilla & Milk Ice Cream Bars

Ben & Jerry's Ice Cream brand

Uncanny Cashew Ice Cream

Cherry Garcia Ice Cream

Coffee For A Change Ice Cream

Butter Pecan Ice Cream

Vanilla For A Change Ice Cream

New York Super Fudge Chunk Ice Cream

Phish Food Ice Cream

Pistachio Ice Cream

Chunky Monkey Ice Cream

Karamel Sutra Ice Cream

Fudge Central Ice Cream

Peanut Butter Me Up Ice Cream

One Sweet Whirled Cream

Cherry Garcia Yogurt

Ben & Jerry's Ice Cream Bars

Cherry Garcia Ice Cream Bars, three-packs

One Sweet Whirled Ice Cream Bars

Always read the labels. At the current time, all theses items are gluten-free.

GLUTEN-FREE RECIPES

SALAD DRESSINGS

THOUSAND ISLAND DRESSING

4 eggs

1 cup canola mayonnaise or Nasoya Nayonaise (gluten-free)

¼ cup Annie's Ketchup (gluten-free)

1-teaspoon pepper

Hard boil eggs. Cut eggs up into very fine pieces. Mix all ingredients together in a bowl. Chill for 15 minutes.

BARBEQUE SALAD DRESSING

1 cup canola mayonnaise or Nasoya Nayonaise (gluten-free)

¼ cup barbecue sauce (gluten-free)

1 tablespoon onion flake

1 tablespoon lemon juice

¼ teaspoon salt

¼ teaspoon pepper

Mix all the ingredients together in a bowl. Chill for 15 minutes.

FETA SALAD DRESSING

¼ cup milk

1 sprig rosemary

¼ cup Boar's Head feta cheese (gluten-free)

1/8 cup olive oil

Salt to taste

Fresh ground pepper to taste

Mix all the ingredients together in a bowl. Chill for 15 minutes.

CREAMY ITALIAN SALAD DRESSING

¼ cup canola mayonnaise or Nasoya Nayonaise (gluten-free)

1 tablespoon milk

1 tablespoon cider vinegar

½ teaspoon oregano

½ teaspoon basil

1/8 teaspoon rosemary

¼ teaspoon sugar

¼ teaspoon garlic powder

1/8 teaspoon garlic salt

1/8 teaspoon pepper

Mix all the ingredients together in a bowl. Chill for 15 minutes.

GREEK SALAD DRESSING

1 clove garlic, minced

¾ teaspoon salt

1 dash pepper

½ cup olive oil

4 tablespoons red wine vinegar

3 tablespoons oregano

Mix all the ingredients together in a bowl. Chill for 15 minutes.

CITRUS SALAD DRESSING

2 tablespoons orange juice

1 tablespoon lemon juice

½ tablespoon Dijon mustard (gluten-free)

½ tablespoon white sugar

2 teaspoons olive oil

Mix all ingredients together in a bowl. Chill for 15 minutes.

RASPBERRY VINAIGRETTE SALAD DRESSING

2 tablespoons raspberry vinegar

1/8 teaspoon salt to taste

1 teaspoon fresh ground pepper

1/3 cup grape seed oil or canola oil

Mix all the ingredients together in a bowl. Chill for 15 minutes.

HONEY FRENCH SALAD DRESSING

1 cup sugar

1 cup ketchup (Annie's gluten-free ketchup)

1 ½ cups oil

½ cup vinegar

1 ½ teaspoons salt

1 ½ teaspoons paprika

1 ½ teaspoons celery seeds

1 onion, chopped

1 tablespoon honey (gluten-free)

Mix all the ingredients together in a bowl. Chill for 15 minutes.

HOUSTON'S HONEY MUSTARD SALAD DRESSING

1 cup olive oil

¼ cup cider vinegar

6 ounces Dijon mustard (1 ½ cups) (gluten-free)

1 dash garlic salt

¾ cup canola mayonnaise or Nasoya Nayonaise (gluten-free)

1 1/8 cups honey (gluten-free)

Mix all the ingredients together in a bowl. Chill for 15 minutes.

SALADS

CHICKEN BLT SALAD

6 cups chopped green salad

2 cups chicken, cut up, cooked

8 slices bacon, cooked crisp and crumbled

2 large tomatoes, sliced

1 hard-boiled egg, sliced

Barbeque Salad Dressing

½ cup canola mayonnaise or Nasoya Nayonaise (gluten-free)

¼ cup barbecue sauce (gluten-free)

1 tablespoon chopped onions

1 tablespoon lemon juice

¼ teaspoon salt

¼ teaspoon pepper

Mix all the ingredients together in a bowl. Chill for 15 minutes.

SPINACH, PEAR, AND WALNUT SALAD

¼ cup honey (gluten-free)

1 tablespoon balsamic vinegar (gluten-free)

2 Pear, preferably corolla pears

¼ cup walnuts

8 cups baby spinach leaves

6 chives, coarsely chopped

Dressing

¼ cup milk

1 sprig rosemary

1/8 cup olive oil

¼ cup soft feta, crumbled (Boar's head) (gluten-free)

Salt and pepper to taste

Mix all the ingredients together in a bowel. Chill for 15 minutes.

GREEK SALAD

8 cups green leaf lettuce, chopped

½ cup purple onion, chopped

1 cup feta cheese (Boar's Head) (gluten-free)

¼ cup olives

5 Pepperoni peppers

Dressing

1 clove garlic, ground finely

¾ teaspoon salt

½ cup olive oil

4 tablespoons red wine vinegar (gluten-free)

3 tablespoons oregano

Mix all the salad dressing ingredients together in a salad dressing mix container.

Mix salad dressing and all ingredients together.

CALIFORNIA PIZZA CHOPPED SALAD

½ head iceberg lettuce, chopped into 1/8-inch wide strips

½ head romaine lettuce, chopped into 1/8-inch wide strips

12 basil leaves, chopped into fine strips

3 cups mozzarella cheese (Boar's head) (gluten-free)

1 cup purple onion

1 cup garbanzo beans

4 cups ripe tomatoes, seeded and diced

3 cups Boar's Head turkey breast, diced (gluten-free)

½ cup Boar's Head salami (gluten-free)

Dressing

1 teaspoon minced fresh garlic

2 teaspoons fresh shallots

2 tablespoons Dijon mustard (Annie's gluten-free)

1 ½ teaspoons oregano

2 teaspoons parsley

½ teaspoon salt

¼ cup red wine vinegar

1 1/3 cups olive oil

3 tablespoons Boar's Head grated parmesan cheese (gluten-free)

Mix all the ingredients together in a salad dressing mixing container.

Mix salad dressing and salad together in a large bowl. Chill for 15 minutes.

TUNA SALAD

1 head iceberg lettuce, peeled

1 cup purple onions, chopped

1 cup cheddar cheese (Boar's head) (gluten-free)

2 cans Wild Oats natural solid white albacore tuna in water or gluten-free

1 tomato, sliced

1 cup canola mayonnaise or Nasoya nayonaise (gluten-free)

¼ cup barbecue sauce (gluten-free)

Lay peeled lettuce out on a large plate. Slice tomatoes and place around the lettuce. Mix all the ingredients together in a large bowl. Scoop tuna mix over the lettuce in the middle. Chill for 15 minutes.

EGG SALAD

5 eggs, hard boiled

1 cup canola mayonnaise or Nasoya nayonaise (gluten-free)

Salt and pepper to taste

1 cup cheddar cheese (Boar's head) (gluten-free)

Peal eggs from shell, cut in half, and remove yoke. Place yoke in a bowl with all the ingredients. Mix all the ingredients together. Fill egg halves with yoke and chill for 15 minutes.

TOMATO SALAD

5 red tomatoes

2 pounds shredded mozzarella cheese (Boar's head) (gluten-free)

Gluten-free balsamic vinaigrette dressing

Cut tomatoes up into slices into a bowl. Mix cheese and dressing together in the bowl. Chill for 15 minutes.

MUSTARD POTATO SALAD

1 ½ pounds white potatoes, peeled

1 ½ cups canola mayonnaise or Nasoya nayonaise (gluten-free)

1 tablespoon gluten-free mustard

1 tablespoon white vinegar

1 teaspoon salt

¼ teaspoon pepper

2 medium celery stalks, chopped (1 cup)

1 medium onion, chopped (½ cup)

4 eggs, hard-cooked chopped

Boil potatoes. Cut potatoes in cubes. Mix all ingredients together in a large bowl. Refrigerate for 1 hour.

GRILLED CHICKEN SALAD

4 boneless skinless chicken breasts

3 cups canola mayonnaise or Nasoya nayonaise (gluten-free)

1 cup purple onions, chopped

1 cup celery, chopped

1 teaspoon salt

¼ teaspoon pepper

1 cup shredded cheddar cheese (Boar's Head) (gluten-free)

Cook chicken on the grill or broil it. Put some gluten-free seasoning on it while cooking it. Cut chicken up into small pieces. Mix all ingredients together in a bowl. Refrigerate for 1 hour.

SOUTHWEST POTATO SALAD

4 unpeeled medium round red potatoes

1 cup canola mayonnaise or Nasoya Nayonaise (gluten-free)

2 tablespoons milk

1 teaspoon cumin seed

1 teaspoon salt

1 large red pepper, chopped

½ cup green onions chopped

Boil red potatoes and then cut into medium pieces.

Mix all the ingredients together in a bowl. Refrigerate for 1 hour.

GREEN BEAN SALAD

1 pound green beans, cut in half

2 tablespoons butter

1 teaspoon grated lemon peel

¼ teaspoon pepper

2 tablespoons pine nuts

Boil green beans for 8 to 10 minutes. Drain water.

Melt butter in saucepan over low heat. Stir in pine nuts. Stir constantly until butter is golden brown. Pour over green beans in a bowl. Toss green beans in sauce. Sprinkle with lemon peels. Then serve.

SANTA FE SALAD

2 cups tortilla strips, crumbled (gluten-free Green Mountain tortilla strips)

3 cups bite-size iceberg lettuce

3 cups bite-size romaine lettuce

1 large tomato, chopped

1 cup shredded cheddar cheese

¼ cup sliced ripe olives

2 tablespoons jalapeno peppers, chopped

1 Jar Green Mountain salsa (gluten-free)

½ cup purple onions, chopped

Mix all ingredients together in a bowl. Chill for 15 minutes.

CORN SALAD

4 cups bite-size mixed salad greens

½ cup yellow corn (gluten-free)

1 red pepper, chopped

½ cup shredded cheddar cheese (Boar's Head) (gluten-free)

¼ cup onion, chopped

1 cup balsamic vinaigrette (gluten-free)

Mix all the ingredients together in a bowl. Chill for 15 minutes.

THREE-BEAN SALAD

4 cups green beans, boiled

4 cups yellow green beans, boiled

1 can gluten-free kidney beans

1 cup fresh red pepper, diced

1 cup green pepper, diced

2 tablespoons parsley, finely minced

1 cup red onion, chopped

½ cup white vinegar (gluten-free)

1/3 cup sugar

1 cup canola oil

1 teaspoon ground pepper

Cut green beans into small pieces. Heat together vinegar, sugar, and onion. Cool and add oil. Pour over all remaining ingredients. Chill several hours.

BEEF AND VEGETABLE SALAD

6 ounces of Boar's Head Deli Roast Beef cut into ½-inch
strips (gluten-free)

2 medium carrots, thinly sliced (1 cup)

1 cup cauliflower

¼ cup sliced radishes

½ cup shredded Monterey Jack cheese (Boar's Head) (gluten-free)

½ cup gluten-free Italian dressing

1 small head iceberg lettuce, chopped in pieces)

Place all ingredients together in a bowl. Mix ingredients together in the bowl.
Let stand 5 minutes.

CUB SALAD

6 cups bite-size iceberg lettuce

1 ½ cups chicken, cut-up, cooked

1 medium tomato, cut into eighths

1/2 cup gluten-free thousand island dressing

1/3 cup cooked bacon, sliced into tiny bites

1 egg, hard boiled, sliced

Toss all ingredients except egg slices in large bowl.
Garnish with egg slices.

STEAK SALAD

1 pound beef boneless top sirloin steak, grilled or broiled, cut into 1 to 1 ½ inches thick

2 medium green onions, thinly sliced

(2 tablespoons)

1 large red pepper, chopped finely

¼ teaspoon salt

1/8 teaspoon pepper

6 cups salad greens, bite-size pieces

1 cup sliced mushrooms

3 cups gluten-free garlic Italian dressing

Place all ingredients together in a bowl. Mix together chill for 5 minutes.

TURKEY SALAD

1 ½ pounds smoked Boar's Head turkey (gluten-free), cut into ¼-inch strips

1 cup shredded Swiss cheese (Boar's Head) (gluten-free)

2 cups seedless red grapes (cut in half)

1 ½ cups almonds

1 ¼ cups canola mayonnaise or Nasoya Nayonaise (gluten-free)

Salt and pepper to taste

Mix all ingredients together in a large bowl. Chill for 5 minutes.

CAESAR SHRIMP SALAD

4 cups cooked gluten-free pasta

1 cup shredded parmesan cheese (Boar's Head) (gluten-free)

1 cup gluten-free creamy Caesar dressing

½ cup purple onions (chopped finely)

1 pound cooked shrimp

7 cups romaine lettuce, chopped

2 cups gluten-free croutons

Mix pasta, cheese, dressing, onions, and shrimp in very large bowl. Toss. Add lettuce and croutons. Serve.

PEPPERONI PASTA SALAD

1 bag of gluten-free pasta, boiled

1 bag of Boar's Head pepperoni (gluten-free)

1 small purple onion, chopped

1 red pepper, chopped

3 cups shredded cheddar cheese (Boar's Head) (gluten-free)

1 bottle of gluten-free balsamic vinaigrette salad dressing

Mix all the ingredients together in a large bowl. Stir well. Chill for 20 minutes, then serve.

CREAMY COLESLAW

1 large bag of coleslaw mix

3 teaspoon gluten-free seasoning (Magic seasoning)

4 cups canola mayonnaise or Nasoya nayonaise (gluten-free)

Black pepper to taste

Toss all ingredients together in a large bowl. Stir well. Chill for 1 hour.

TEXAS COLESLAW

1 bag coleslaw mix

½ cup chopped fresh cilantro

2 cans mexicorn whole-kernel corn (gluten-free), drained

¼ cup canola oil

3 tablespoons lime or lemon juice

¾ teaspoon ground cumin

½ teaspoon salt

Toss all ingredients together in a large bowl.
Chill for 1 hour.

GERMAN POTATO SALAD

2 pounds red potatoes

8 slices bacon, chopped

1 Medium onion, finely chopped

½ teaspoon sugar

½ cup white vinegar (gluten-free)

1 tablespoon spicy mustard (gluten-free)

¼ teaspoon black pepper

¼ cup chopped fresh parsley leaves

Boil potatoes in a large saucepan add 1 tablespoon of salt. Bring to a boil until they become tender

Reserve ½ cup potato cooking water.

Fry bacon. Reserve ¼ cup bacon grease. Add ¼ bacon grease in a skillet. Add onions cook until softened and beginning to brown. Stir in the sugar until dissolved. Add the vinegar and reserve potato cooking water. Bring to a simmer. Add potatoes, parsley, and chopped bacon to the skillet and toss to combine. Add the seasoning with salt to taste. Serve immediately while still warm.

TOMATO CUCUMBER SALAD

2 medium cucumbers, sliced and peeled

5 large tomatoes, sliced

¼ cup onion, finely chopped

3 cups roasted garlic vinaigrette salad dressing (gluten-free)

Mix all the ingredients together in a large bowl. Chill for 30 minutes.

GLUTEN-FREE SEASONING FOR COOKING

I have listed all the seasoning companies below that have gluten-free seasoning with the company name and phone number. Call them to find the local retailer in your area.

Steak Dance Meat Seasoning & Tenderizer
812-476-5040

The Spice Hunter
(big selection of seasoning)
800-444-3061

Wild Oats Natural Seasoning
Poultry Seasoning
Beef & Pork Seasoning
Fish & Seafood Seasoning
Chicken Seasoning

Bone Suckin' Sauce Rub
(big selection of seasoning)
800-446-0947

Magic Seasoning Mail Order
(big selection of seasoning)
800-457-2857

Call the numbers on the list above and order your favorite gluten-free
seasoning for cooking.

SIDE DISHES

NACO CHEESE CHIPS

1 bag Wild Oats natural white corn tortilla or 1 bag Green mountain gringo tortilla strips (gluten-free)

1 can Amy's organic chili (gluten-free)

1 purple onion, chopped

1 red pepper, chopped

2 jalapenos, sliced

1 cup shredded mild cheddar cheese (Boar's Head) (gluten-free)

Lay the chips out on large plate. Place all the ingredients over the chips. Heat in a microwave for 2 minutes.

CORN CASSEROLE

3 cans gluten-free canned whole kernel corn

½ cup onion, chopped

2 tablespoons gluten-free seasoning (Magic Chef)

3 cups Imagine organic Creamy Sweet Corn Soup (gluten-free)

2 cups gluten-free shredded sharp cheddar cheese

¼ cup Gillian's foods Italian bread crumbs (gluten-free)

Mix everything together in a large casserole dish. Stir all the ingredients together. Bake for 15 minutes in the oven at 425.

GREEN BEAN CASSEROLE

1 bag of fresh cut green beans

1 red pepper, chopped

1 purple onion, chopped

¼ cup Gillian's foods Italian bread crumbs (gluten-free)

1 stick butter

2 tablespoons Magic seasoning salt (gluten-free)

In a large frying pan, melt the butter and add all the ingredients together. Mix together. Fry until green beans are tender.

BROCCOLI CHEESE CASSEROLE

1 bag of fresh broccoli, chopped

1 purple onion, chopped

1 red pepper, chopped

½ cup shredded cheddar cheese (Boar's Head) (gluten-free)

3 tablespoons of Magic seasoning

1 stick butter

In a large frying pan, melt the butter and add the broccoli and seasoning. Fry until the broccoli is tender. In a large casserole dish, add broccoli and all remaining ingredients. Stir well and bake for 15 minutes at 425.

DEVIL EGGS

1 dozen eggs, boiled or hard boiled

2 tablespoons Streak Dance seasoning

½ cup sharp shredded cheddar cheese (Boar's Head) (gluten-free)

1 tablespoon black pepper

1 cup Nasoya Nayonaise or canola mayonnaise (gluten-free)

Cut eggs in half and remove yoke. Place egg halves on a large dish. Place egg yokes in a large mixing bowl. Mix all ingredients together. Scoop up mix and fill the eggs with mix. Chill for 20 minutes.

BARBEQUE BAKED BEANS

1 can navy beans (gluten-free)

1 can small red beans (gluten-free)

1 can pinto beans (gluten-free)

½ pound bacon, fried and crumbled

½ onions, chopped

1 cup Bone suckin' BBQ Sauce (gluten-free)

½ cup Annie's gluten-free ketchup

2 tablespoons brown sugar

1 tablespoon vinegar (gluten-free)

¼ cup Annie's mustard (gluten-free)

Drain and rinse beans. Put in two-quart baking dish. Stir remaining ingredients and mix well with a large spoon. Cover and bake at 350 for 1 hour.

MASH POTATOES WITH GRAVY

1 bag Idaho potatoes, peeled and boiled

32 ounces Imagine organic creamy potato soup (gluten-free)

½ cup onion, chopped finely

5 tablespoons Bob's red mill white rice flour (gluten –free)

Boil potatoes and mash with milk and butter to taste.

Place potato soup and chopped onions in a large sauce. Bring to a boil. Add Bob's Red Mill white rice flour (gluten-free) to thicken up the mix.

CORN BREAD STUFFING

1 Loft corn bread gluten-free bread (sliced in little bite-size pieces)
Wild Oats store

1 onion, chopped

1 ½ pounds ground beef

32 ounces Imagine organic beef broth gluten-free

3 tablespoons steak dance seasoning gluten-free

In a large frying pan, brown beef and onions. In a large casserole dish, place the beef and all ingredients together. Mix well together until bread is soft. Bake for 20 minutes at 350.

NACHO CHEESE DIP

3 pounds Boar's Head cheddar cheese

1 bag of Wild Oats natural white corn tortilla chips or Green Mountain gringo tortilla strips gluten-free

½ jar Green Mountain salsa or fresh salsa (gluten-free)

In a large sauce pot, melt cheese and add salsa.

TOMATO SALSA DIP

1 bag of wild oats natural white corn tortilla chips or green mountain gringo tortilla strips gluten-free

1 ½ pounds firm, ripe tomatoes, cut into 3/8 inch dice (About 3 cups)

1 jalapeno chile seeds and ribs removed, minced

½ cup minced red onion

¼ cup chopped fresh cilantro leaves

½ teaspoon salt pinch of pepper

5 teaspoons fresh lime juice

Sugar to taste

In a large bowl, mix all the ingredients together.

MEAT AND CHEESE BITES

½ pound Boar's Head salami (gluten-free)

½ pound Boar's Head Swiss cheese (gluten-free)

Carrots, sliced

Red pepper, sliced

On each of the toothpicks, alternate pieces of salami, vegetables, and cheese.

SALAMI BAKED RED PEPPERS

4 red peppers, sliced into sixteen quarters

16 slices of Boar's Head mozzarella (gluten-free)

16 slices of Boar's Head salami (gluten-free)

Magic seasoning salt

Lay out the red pepper on a baking tray. Place salami, cheese, and Magic seasoning salt on top of the peppers. Bake for 20 minutes on 350.

SAUTÉED ONIONS AND RED PEPPERS

4 red peppers, sliced

4 purple onions, sliced

¼ cup olive oil

3 tablespoons Magic seasoning salt

In a large frying pan, sauté the onions and peppers in the olive oil until they are soft. Then they are ready to serve.

SPICY LEMON SHRIMP COCKTAIL

1 tablespoon grated lemon peel

3 tablespoons fresh lemon juice

¾ teaspoon crushed red pepper flakes

½ teaspoon salt

2 garlic cloves, finely chopped

2 tablespoons olive oil

1 pound uncooked large shrimp

½ cup fresh basil leaves, finely chopped

½ cup canola mayonnaise or Nasoya Nayonaise (gluten-free)

In a medium glass bowl, mix lemon peel, lemon juice, red pepper flakes, salt, garlic, and 1 tablespoon of oil. Add shrimp. Toss to coat.

In an un-greased pan, spread shrimp out. Broil for 5 minutes until shrimp are pink.

Add mayonnaise and basil and the remaining oil together in a food processor. Process until smooth. Serve with shrimp and mayonnaise.

FRESH MOZZARELLA AND TOMATO

4 medium tomatoes

8 ounces fresh mozzarella cheese, cut into slices (gluten-free)

2 tablespoon olive oil

2 tablespoons balsamic

2 tablespoons chopped fresh basil leaves

Freshly ground pepper

On round plate, arrange tomato and cheese slices alternately. Drizzle oil and balsamic over tomatoes. Sprinkle with basil and pepper.

Chill for 20 minutes.

BRUSCHETTA

1 loaf French bread gluten-free band, sliced

2 tablespoons olive oil

5 Small plum (roma tomatoes)

8 OZ fresh mozzarella cheese (gluten-free)

1/2 lb thinly sliced Boar's Head salami (gluten-free)

½ medium green onions, sliced

2 tablespoons extra-virgin olive oil

2 tablespoons balsamic

2 tablespoons chopped fresh basil leaves

Heat oven to 375. Brush both sides of the bread slices with olive oil. Place on un-greased cookie sheet. Bake 5 minutes or until crisp. Cool 5 minutes.

Meanwhile, cut each tomato into 6 slices. Place cheese, tomato, onions, salami over each bread slice.

Mix oil and balsamic vinegar. Drizzle over the top of the bread. Sprinkle with basil.

SAUTÉED POTATOES

5 large potatoes, chopped in medium-size pieces

1 medium white onion, finely chopped

4 tablespoons Magic seasoning salt

1 stick butter

Wash potatoes well and chop into medium pieces.

In a large frying pan, melt butter and sautéed onions with Magic salt and add potatoes and cook to liking.

CHERRY PEPPERS WITH SALAMI AND MOZZARELLA

10 medium cherry peppers, drained and seeded

1 thick slice Boar's Head salami, sliced

4 slices thin Boar's Head mozzarella (gluten-free)

1 bottle olive oil

3 tablespoons balsamic vinegar

Clean out the seeds out of the center of the cherry peppers. Slice salami to fit the cherry peppers and wrap salami in the mozzarella cheese. Place cheese and salami in the cherry pepper. Place into a large bowl. Add oil and balsamic vinegar. Chill for 4 hours.

MOZZARELLA STICKS

4 slices Boar's Head ham

8 ounces gluten-free mozzarella cheese

Cut the cheese into 4 even-sized pieces. Then roll the cheese up into the ham. Secure each morsel with a toothpick.

Baked on 350 until the cheese is melted.

SWEET POTATO AND APPLE CASSEROLE

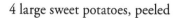

4 large sweet potatoes, peeled

4 small apples

4 tablespoons gluten-free brown sugar

Butter

Slice the sweet potatoes and the apples into a greased casserole dish. Layer potatoes and apples. Sprinkle with butter and brown sugar in between 1 or 2 layers of the casserole.

Bake on 350 for 1 hour.

SOUPS

MEXICAN POTATO SOUP

1 or 2 large potatoes, peeled and cut into cubes (2 cups)

1 cup corn kernels

½ red bell pepper, chopped

½ jalapeno, chopped

½ cup water

1 bag (32 fl. oz.) Imagine organic chicken broth

1 ½ teaspoons cumin

½ teaspoon chili power

Salt and pepper to taste

In medium saucepan combine all ingredients. Simmer covered until potatoes are done—15 to 20 minutes. Add gluten-free white rice flour to thicken. Put shredded cheddar over the top when you put it into the soup bowl.

TACO SOUP

1 pound ground beef

½ cup diced onion

1 cup diced tomatoes

1 can gluten-free tomato sauce

1 can gluten-free red beans, rinsed and drained

1 corn gluten-free whole-kernel corn with liquid

3 teaspoons gluten-free chili power

Brown beef and onion in a frying pan. Drain grease. Put in a large pot.

Add remaining ingredients. Bring to boil. Reduce heat and simmer for 20 minutes.

Ladle soup in bowls. Top each bowl with a handful of crushed gluten-free tortilla chips and a sprinkle of shredded cheese, if desired.

CHICKEN NOODLE SOUP

2 cups cooked chicken, cut-up

2 medium stalks celery, chopped (1 cup)

2 medium carrots, sliced (1 cup)

1 medium onion (Chopped ½ cup)

1 tablespoon chopped fresh parsley

1 teaspoon dried thyme leaves

¼ teaspoon pepper

2 cloves garlic, finely chopped

1 box (32 fl. oz.) Imagine organic chicken broth gluten-free)

1 gluten-free soup noodles

In four-quart saucepan, heat all ingredients except noodles to boiling. Stir in noodles. Heat to boiling; reduce heat.

Simmer uncovered 8 to 10 minutes, stirring occasionally.

CHICKEN CORDON BLEU CHOWDER SOUP

1 bag (32 fl. oz.) Imagine potato soup mix (gluten-free)

1 cup cooked chicken

1 cup cooked ham (Boar's Head) (gluten-free)

1 cup shredded Swiss cheese (Boar's Head) (gluten-free)

1 tablespoon chopped fresh chives

1 teaspoon garlic

In four-quart saucepan, heat soup, chicken, and ham over medium heat for 5 minutes, stirring occasionally.

Slowly stir in cheese. Cook about 2 minutes, stirring frequently, until cheese is melted.

Top with chives.

ITALIAN TOMATO SOUP

1 cup water

2 cups diced tomatoes

1 teaspoon Italian herbs

1 can gluten-free tomato juice

2 tablespoon basil pesto

4 slices gluten-free French bread

2 tablespoons shredded parmesan cheese (Boar's Head) (gluten-free)

In four-quart saucepan, heat water, tomato juice, and tomato, bring a boiling.

Place bread on a cookie sheet. Spread with pesto; sprinkle with cheese. Broil bread until golden brown (1 to 2 minutes)

Ladle soup over bread slices.

SOUTHWEST CHEESE SOUP

1 pound prepared cheese product cut into cubes (Boar's Head) (gluten-free)

1 can gluten-free whole-kernel corn, drained)

1 Can gluten-free black beans, drained and rinsed

1 cup diced tomatoes

1 green chilies, chopped

1 cup milk

In four-quart saucepan, mix all ingredients.

Cook over medium-low heat 10 to 15 minutes, stirring frequently, until cheese is melted and soup is hot.

VEGETABLE BEEF SOUP

1 pound boneless beef sirloin steak, cut into ½-inch cubes

1 bag frozen mixed vegetables

1 can plain gluten-free tomato sauce

1 box (32 fl. oz.) Imagine organic beef broth (gluten-free)

2 cans spicy hot gluten-free vegetable juice

Cook beef in skillet for about 10 minutes, stirring occasionally.

In three-quart saucepan stir remaining ingredients. Heat to boiling. Reduce heat. Cover. Simmer 5 minutes, stirring occasionally.

ZESTY PORK SOUP

1 pound pork tenderloin, cut into 1-inch cubes

2 medium dark-orange sweet potatoes, peeled and cut in cubes

2 cloves garlic, finely chopped

2 teaspoons ginger root, finely chopped

1 box (32 fl. oz.) Imagine organic chicken broth (gluten-free)

2 cups water

2 tablespoons gluten-free soy sauce

2 cups uncooked gluten-free soup noodles, boiled

1 medium carrot, sliced

1 small red bell pepper, chopped

2 cups fresh spinach leaves

In large frying pan, cook pork, garlic, and gingerroot. Cook 3 to 5 minutes, stirring frequently until pork is brown.

In a four-quart saucepan, stir remaining ingredients together. Bring to a boil. Simmer uncovered for about 10 minutes.

MOZZARELLA BEEF VEGGIE SOUP

1 pound lean ground beef

1 large onion, chopped

1 cup diced tomatoes

½ cup green peppers, chopped

½ cup celery, chopped

2 cups mixed vegetables

4 cups water

1 cup Imagine organic beef broth (gluten-free)

1 ½ teaspoons Italian seasoning (gluten-free)

¼ teaspoon pepper

1 cup shredded mozzarella cheese (Boar's Head) (gluten-free)

In a large frying pan, brown beef.

Stir remaining ingredients except cheese. Heat to a boil; reduce heat. Simmer uncovered for 10 minutes.

Sprinkle cheese onto soup bowl serving.

MAIN DISHES

CHICKEN AND CORN QUICHE

1 gluten-free pie crust (Gillian's pie crust)

6 eggs

2 cups shredded cheddar cheese (Boar's Head) (gluten-free)

2 cups chicken, cooked

1 small onion, finely chopped

2 tablespoons Spice Hunter vegetable seasoning

1 medium red pepper, finely chopped

Mix all ingredients together in a large bowl. Stir well.

Pour into pie shell. Bake at 375 for 15 minutes.

BROCCOLI QUICHE

1 gluten-free pie crust (Gillian's pie crust)

6 eggs

2 cups shredded cheddar cheese (Boar's Head) (gluten-free)

2 cups broccoli, finely chopped

1 small onion, finely chopped

2 tablespoons Spice Hunter vegetable seasoning

1 medium red pepper, finely chopped

Mix all ingredients together in a large bowl. Stir well.

Pour into pie shell. Bake at 375 for 15 minutes.

BLUE CHEESE QUICHE

1 gluten-free pie crust (Gillian's pie crust)

6 eggs

5 ounces Boar's Head gluten-free blue cheese

¼ cup fresh parsley, finely chopped

½ cup ground walnuts

Mix all ingredients together in a large bowl. Stir well.

Pour into pie shell. Bake at 375 for 15 minutes.

HAM AND CHEESE QUICHE

1 gluten-free pie crust (Gillian's pie crust)

6 eggs

2 cups chopped Boar's Head ham (gluten-free)

2 tablespoons Spice Hunter vegetable seasoning

2 cups shredded cheddar cheese (Boar's Head) (gluten free)

Mix all ingredients together in a large bowl. Stir well.

Pour into pie shell. Bake at 375 for 15 minutes.

MEXICAN QUICHE

1 gluten-free pie crust gillian's pie crust

6 Eggs

2 cups shredded cheddar cheese (gluten-free)

1 Medium onion (Finely chopped)

1 cup red peppers (Finely chopped)

½ cup Jalapeno (Finely chopped)

Mix all ingredients together in a large bowl. Stir well

Pour into pie shell. Bake at 375 for 15 minutes.

Top slices with Green Mountain gringo salsa (gluten-free salsa).

SPINACH QUICHE

1 gluten-free pie crust (Gillian's pie crust)

6 eggs

2 cups shredded cheddar cheese (Boar's Head) (gluten-free)

1 medium onion, finely chopped

1 cup red peppers, finely chopped

2 cups spinach, finely chopped

2 tablespoons Spice Hunter vegetable seasoning

Mix all ingredients together in a large bowl. Stir well.

Pour into pie shell. Bake at 375 for 15 minutes.

MEATLOAF

1 pound ground beef

½ pound ground pork

½ onion, finely chopped

½ red pepper, finely chopped

2 garlic cloves, minced

¾ cup gluten-free bread crumbs (Gillian's band)

1 large egg, lightly beaten

¼ cup milk

3 tablespoons gluten-free ketchup

½ teaspoon salt

¼ teaspoon pepper

Mix all ingredients together in a bowl.

Lay out the meat on a meatloaf baking dish.

Bake on 350 for 1 hour 10 minutes.

TOMATO SAUCE MEAT LOAF

1 pound ground beef

½ pound ground pork sausage

½ cup red pepper, finely chopped

½ cup onion, finely chopped

¼ cup gluten-free ketchup

1 large egg, lightly beaten

½ teaspoon salt

¼ teaspoon pepper

1 can gluten-free tomato sauce

Mix all ingredients together in a bowl.

Lay out the meat on a meatloaf baking dish.

Bake on 350 for 1 hour.

Remove meatloaf from the oven. Pour tomato sauce over the meat. Heat for 10 minutes.

TRUCK SHOP MEATLOAF

1 ½ pounds ground pork sausage

½ cup onion, finely chopped

½ cup yellow peppers, finely chopped

½ cup gluten-free tomato juice

1 large egg, lightly beaten

¼ teaspoon salt

Gravy

1 box (32 fl. oz.) Imagine organic beef broth (gluten-free)

4 tablespoons gluten-free white rice flour

Pour the beef broth into a medium sauce pan. Bring to a bowl and add flour to thicken the gravy.

Lay out the meat on a meatloaf baking dish.

Bake on 350 for 1 hour.

Remove the meatloaf and pour gravy over the meatloaf and heat for 10 minutes.

CLASSIC MEATLOAF

2 pounds ground beef

1 cup onion, finely chopped

1 cup gluten-free bread crumbs (Gillian's bread crumbs)

2 large eggs, lightly beaten

3 tablespoons dry red wine

½ cup Imagine organic beef broth (gluten-free)

½ teaspoon salt

¼ teaspoon pepper

1 can gluten-free tomato sauce

Mix all ingredients together in a bowl.

Lay out the meat on a meatloaf baking dish.

Bake on 350 for 1 hour.

Remove the meatloaf and pour the tomato sauce over the meatloaf and heat for 10 minutes.

CHEESEBURGER MEATLOAF

1 ¼ pounds ground beef

1 cup sweet onion, finely chopped

2 tablespoons whole milk

1 large egg, lightly beaten

1 cup shredded cheddar cheese

1 tablespoon gluten-free ketchup

1 tablespoon gluten-free mayonnaise

1 tablespoon gluten-free mustard

2 tablespoon Boar's Head sweet pickle relish (gluten-free)

¼ tablespoon salt

¼ tablespoon pepper

Mix the ingredients together in a bowl.

Lay out the meat on a meatloaf baking dish.

Bake on 350 for 1 hour.

SPANISH MEATLOAF

1 ½ pounds ground beef

½ package frozen spinach finely chopped

¼ cup onion, finely chopped

1 garlic clove, minced

2 tablespoons parsley, chopped

½ cup freshly grated parmesan (Boar's Head) (gluten-free)

¼ cup whole milk

¼ teaspoon salt

¼ teaspoon pepper

Mix the ingredients together in a bowl.

Lay out the meat on a meat loaf baking dish

Bake on 350 for 1 hour.

MEXICAN MEATLOAF

1 ½ pound ground beef

1/2 cup gluten-free tortilla chips, crushed

1 cup onion, finely chopped

½ cup green pepper, finely chopped

2 garlic cloves, minced

1 cup corn kernels

2 tablespoons parsley, chopped

1 ½ cups fresh tomato salsa (gluten-free)

1 large egg, lightly beaten

½ teaspoon dried oregano

½ teaspoon salt

¼ teaspoon pepper

Mix the ingredients together in a bowl.

Lay out the meat on a meatloaf baking dish.

Bake on 350 for 1 hour.

MASHED POTATO MEATLOAF

1 pound ground beef

½ pound ground pork sausage

1 garlic clove, minced

½ cup gluten-free tomato juice

2 tablespoons gluten-free ketchup

1 large egg, lighten beaten

½ teaspoon salt

¼ teaspoon pepper

Mashed Potato

1 small bag of potatoes, peeled boiled, mashed in a large bowl

2 cups gluten-free shredded sharp cheddar cheese

Mix all ingredients except the potatoes together in a bowl.

Lay out the meat on a meatloaf baking dish.

Bake on 350 for 1 hour.

Lay mashed potatoes over meatloaf and spread cheese over the potatoes. Bake
for 10 minutes.

PIZZA MEATLOAF

1 ½ Italian pork sausage

¾ gluten-free bread crumbs (Gillian's band)

½ cup green peppers, finely chopped

½ cup yellow onion, finely chopped

1 large egg, lightly beaten

¼ teaspoon dried oregano

¼ teaspoon salt

¼ teaspoon pepper

1 can gluten-free pizza sauce

½ cup sliced mushroom

15 pepperoni slices

¾ cup shredded mozzarella (Boar's Head) (gluten-free)

Mix the ingredients together in a bowl.

Lay out the meat on a meatloaf baking dish.

Bake on 350 for 1 hour.

SLOPPY JOES

2 pounds ground beef

1 medium onion, finely chopped

2 teaspoons Spice Hunter hamburger seasoning

½ cup gluten-free ketchup

1 bag gluten-free hamburger buns

In a large saucepan, brown beef in oil. Add ketchup.

BEEF STEW

1 pound beef, cut in 1-inch cubes

1 tablespoon oil

3 cups Imagine organic beef broth (gluten-free)

½ teaspoon salt

1/8 teaspoon pepper

2 cups potatoes, cubed

1 cup carrots, diced

1 cup celery, chopped

1 small onion, chopped

1 bay leaf

½ cup cold water

2 tablespoon corn starch (Red Mills gluten-free)

In a large saucepan, brown beef in oil. Add broth, salt, and pepper. Heat to a boil. Cover and simmer 2 ½ hours, till beef is almost tender.

Stir in vegetables and bay leaf. Cover and simmer for 30 minutes.

Mix cold water and corn starch together, then gradually stir into stew. Heat to a boil and stir 1 minute more to thicken.

TACOS

2 pounds ground beef

1 medium onion, finely chopped

1 box gluten-free yellow corn shells

3 tablespoon Spice Hunter chili pepper seasoning

1 bag gluten-free shredded cheddar cheese

1 bag shredded lettuce

2 large jalapeno, sliced

1 jar Green Mountain salsa (gluten-free)

Bake taco shells on 450 for 3 minutes.

In a large saucepan, brown beef in oil. Add chili pepper.

VEGGIES AND STEAK

1 pound beef sirloin steak, cut ¾-inch thick

1 package fresh mushrooms

1 large onion (chopped into medium size pieces)

1 cup halved cherry tomatoes

¼ Olive oil

½ cup balsamic vinaigrette (gluten-free)

In a large saucepan, brown beef in the olive oil.

Add all ingredients and balsamic vinaigrette. Mix and heat.

SPAGHETTI

1 package of gluten-free spaghetti noodles, boiled and drained

1 jar gluten-free spaghetti sauce

1 medium onion, chopped

1/3 cup gluten-free grated parmesan cheese (Boar's Head)

Boil noodles.

In a medium sauce pan, add the spaghetti sauce and onions. Bring to a boil.

Mix the noodles and spaghetti sauce together. Top with the grated parmesan cheese.

MEATBALLS

2 pounds ground beef

1 medium onion, chopped

2 tablespoons Spice Hunter Italian seasoning (gluten-free)

3 tablespoons Spice Hunter hamburger seasoning (gluten-free)

2 garlic cloves, minced finely

2 jar gluten-free pasta sauce

½ cup shredded mozzarella (Boar's Head) (Gluten Free)

Mix all ingredients except pasta sauce together.

Roll ground beef into small round balls.

Bake in a casserole dish on 350 for 1 hour.

Pour pasta sauce over the meat and heat for 15 minutes.

Add shredded mozzarella (Boar's Head) (gluten-free).

MEAT LOVER'S PIZZA

1 pound ground beef

½ cup chopped green pepper

1 can gluten-free pizza sauce

1 package gluten-free pepperoni, chopped

¼ cup fresh olives, sliced

2 cup gluten-free shredded mozzarella (Boar's Head)

2 eggs

¾ cup milk

¾ cup gluten-free baking mix

In a large skillet, cook beef and green pepper over medium heat until meat is no longer pink; drain. Stir in the pizza sauce, pepperoni, and olives. Transfer to a greased baking dish (11 x 7 x 2). Sprinkle with cheese.

In a small bowl, combine baking mix , eggs, and milk until blended. Pour evenly over cheese. Bake uncovered at 400 for 25 to 30 minutes or until golden brown.

BEEF TIPS

2 pounds beef stew (sliced into cubes)

1 bag gluten-free white rice

3 tablespoons Spice Hunter beef seasoning (gluten-free)

32 ounces Imagine organic beef broth (gluten-free)

1 large onion, chopped

4 tablespoons olive oil

In a large fry pan, add the beef and onions and seasoning. Brown beef. Add beef broth and bring to a broil.

Broil rice and drain.

In a large casserole dish, lay rice out. Pour beef and broth over the rice.

ITALIAN BEEF

2 pounds brisket, finely chopped

3 tablespoons Spice Hunter beef seasoning (gluten-free)

2 medium onions, chopped

2 (32 fl. oz.) Imagine organic beef broth

3 tablespoons olive oil

1 loaf gluten-free French bread

In a large frying pan, lightly brown the brisket.

In a large saucepan, add beef, seasoning, and beef broth. Bring to a broil and simmer for 30 minutes. Serve with French bread.

ITALIAN SAUSAGE LASAGNA

1 pound Italian sausage

1 medium green bell pepper, chopped

1 small package mushrooms, sliced

3 cups gluten-free small lasagna noodles

2 ½ cups water

½ teaspoon Spice Hunter Italian seasoning (gluten-free)

1 jar pasta sauce (gluten free)

1 cup shredded gluten-free mozzarella cheese (Boar's Head)

In twelve-inch skillet cook sausage, bell pepper, mushrooms, and onions over medium heat, stirring occasionally, until sausage is no longer pink.

Stir in remaining ingredients except cheese. Heat to boiling, stirring occasionally; reduce heat. Simmer uncovered about 10 minutes or until pasta is tender. Sprinkle with cheese.

BEEF STIR FRY

1 pound boneless beef sirloin

2 cups water

3 ounces Imagine organic beef broth (gluten-free)

1 cup broccoli, sliced

1 cup carrots, sliced

1 medium onion, chopped

1 red bell pepper, chopped

2 teaspoons Spice Hunter stir fry seasoning (gluten-free)

3 tablespoons oil

Cut beef into strips. Add 3 tablespoons of olive oil in a twelve-inch skillet; heat over medium heat until beef is brown.

In the same skillet, heat water to boiling. Add vegetables, seasoning. Boil for 5 minutes, until vegetables are tender.

BOWTIE PASTA, BEEF, AND TOMATOES

2 cups uncooked gluten-free bowtie pasta

1 tablespoon olive oil

1 cup green bell pepper, chopped

1 pound beef strips, thinly sliced

1 can gluten-free Italian stewed tomatoes

1 teaspoon fresh garlic, finely chopped

2 teaspoons fresh basil, finely chopped

2 cups gluten-free shredded parmesan cheese

1 teaspoon salt

1 teaspoon pepper

Cook and drain pasta.

In a large skillet, heat oil over medium heat. Cook bell pepper, beef, garlic, and oil until beef is brown.

Stir in tomatoes, salt, and pepper. Cook 3 minutes, stirring frequently. Stir in pasta. Add basil and cheese. Heat for 2 minutes.

BARBECUED BEEF RIBS

½ cup Bone Suckin' sauce rib rub (gluten-free)

5 pounds beef ribs

2 jars Bone Suckin' barbecued sauce, hot (gluten-free)

1 small onion (finely chopped)

In a casserole dish, lay ribs out. Add rib rub and barbecue sauce over the ribs. Bake for 1 hour at 375.

BEEF BRISKET

5 pounds beef brisket

32 ounces Imagine beef broth (gluten-free)

3 medium onions, finely chopped

½ cup water

1 tablespoon salt

1 tablespoon pepper

In a large baking pot, put all ingredients together. Cover baking pot and heat on 375 for 2 ½ hours or till beef is tender.

BEEF SHEPHERD'S PIE

2 cups fresh mashed potatoes

1 tablespoon olive oil

1 large egg, lightly beaten

2 pounds ground beef

1 medium onion, finely chopped

1 cup shredded cheddar cheese (Boar's Head) (gluten-free)

Brown beef in a large skillet with onions and olive oil. Cook until brown.

In a large casserole dish, add beef and lay potatoes over the beef. Add shredded cheddar cheese over the potatoes. Bake for 15 minutes.

POT ROAST

4 pounds boneless beef chuck roast

1 tablespoon chopped rosemary

1 teaspoon Spice Hunter paprika seasoning

1 tablespoon salt

1 tablespoon pepper

2 tablespoons olive oil

1 cup Imagine organic beef broth (gluten-free)

5 cups small onions, finely chopped

3 garlic cloves, finely chopped

1 pound carrots

3 potatoes, sliced

In a large casserole dish, place chuck roast and add all ingredients. Bake on 375 for 45 minutes. Keep basting the roast to keep it tender. Make sure beef is fully cooked.

MINI·PIZZA

gluten-free pizza crust (kinnikinnick)

1 can gluten-free pizza sauce

2 cups of gluten-free mozzarella cheese

Use your favorite toppings, for example, onions, peppers, pepperoni, sausage, ham, etc.

Bake at 350 for 10 minutes.

ANTIPASTO FRENCH BREAD

1 loaf gluten-free French bread

¼ cup basil pesto

10 slices Boar's Head salami (gluten-free)

3 plum tomatoes, thinly sliced

1 small green bell pepper, cut in thin rings

2 medium onions, chopped

¼ cup sliced ripe olives

6 slices Boar's Head provolone cheese (gluten-free)

Bake on 425. Place bread halves, cut sides up, on un-greased cookie sheet. Spread with pesto. Top with salami, tomatoes, bell peppers, onions, olives, and cheese.

Bake for 10 minutes until cheese is melted.

TACO CHICKEN

1 cup Spice Hunter chili pepper seasoning (gluten-free)

2 tablespoons olive oil

4 boneless skinless chicken breasts

1 can whole-kernel corn (gluten-free)

1 small red bell pepper, chopped

1 small onion, finely chopped

1 tablespoon lime juice

In medium bowl coat chicken with chili pepper seasoning.

In large skillet heat oil over medium heat. Cook chicken in oil for 3 to 5 minutes. Add remaining ingredients to skillet. Cook for 8 minutes over medium heat. Stir well.

TUSCAN CHICKEN AND WHITE BEANS

1/3 cup gluten-free Italian dressing

4 boneless skinless chicken breasts

¼ cup water

2 cups celery, sliced

2 cups carrots, sliced

¼ cup sun-dried tomatoes in oil

1 teaspoon dried rosemary leaves

1 can gluten-free cannelloni beans, drained and rinsed

In a large skillet, heat dressing over medium heat. Cook chicken in dressing for 3 minutes on each side or until lightly browned.

Reduce heat to low. Add water, celery, carrots, tomatoes, and rosemary to skillet. Cover and simmer for about 10 minutes.

Stir in beans. Cover and cook for 6 minutes.

ROASTED CHICKEN

1 small onion (finely chopped)

32 ounces Imagine organic onion soup broth (gluten-free)

2 tablespoons olive oil

2 tablespoons lemon juice

3 ½ pounds roasting chicken

In a large plastic bag, combine soup mix blended with oil and lemon juice; add chicken. Close bag and shake. Cover and marinate in refrigerator. Turn occasionally for 2 hours.

Remove from the plastic bag and place in a baking dish. Bake at 350 for 1 hour 20 minutes or until meat thermometer reaches 180 F. Baste chicken with juices every 20 minutes.

BLUE CHEESE STUFFED CHICKEN BREASTS

½ cup crumbled blue cheese (Boar's Head gluten-free)

2 whole boneless chicken breast with skin (not split)

2 tablespoons butter

1 tablespoon fresh lemon juice

½ teaspoon Spice Hunter paprika seasoning (gluten-free)

1 teaspoon dried thyme

Mix blue cheese, seasonings, and lemon juice together.

Split chicken in the center. Stuff chicken with blue cheese mix.

Grill chicken for 7 minutes on each side or until cooked.

BARBECUE MUSHROOM CHICKEN

1 pound boneless skinless chicken breast

1 small onion, chopped

1 package fresh mushrooms, sliced

1 cup Bone Suckin' barbecue sauce (gluten-free)

1 box of white rice (gluten-free)

Heat 2 tablespoons oil in a large skillet over medium-high heat.

Cook chicken in the skillet 5 minutes on each side until fully cooked.

Remove the chicken from the skillet.

In the same skillet, add mushrooms, onions, and sauté them. Add barbecue sauce. Heat and place chicken back into the skillet.

Serve with some gluten-free white rice.

LEMON GARLIC CHICKEN

4 boneless, skinless chicken breast halves

1 large red pepper, chopped

½ teaspoon Spice Hunter paprika seasoning (gluten-free)

¼ teaspoon ground pepper

2 tablespoon butter

2 teaspoons lemon juice

1 garlic clove, finely chopped

1 box white rice (gluten-free)

In a large skillet, add all ingredients and cook for 5 minutes on each side over medium heat until chicken is done.

Serve with gluten-free white rice.

CHICKEN & CORN

1 teaspoon Spice Hunter chili powder seasoning (gluten-free)

½ teaspoon salt

2 tablespoons olive oil

1 cup onions, chopped

2 medium red peppers, chopped

1 medium green pepper, chopped

4 boneless chicken breasts

2 teaspoons Gluten-free hot pepper sauce

1 package frozen whole-kernel corn (thawed)

Combine chili power and salt in shallow dish. Add chicken. Turn to coat.

Heat one teaspoon oil in large skillet on medium heat. Add chicken. Cook for 5 minutes on each side until done.

Heat remaining ingredients with 2 tablespoons olive oil. Cook and stir 2 minutes or until tender.

LEMON PEPPER CHICKEN

4 chicken quarters (about 2 ½ pounds)

¾ teaspoon salt

2 teaspoons grated lemon peel

3 cloves garlic, minced

1 tablespoon cracked black pepper

1 tablespoon gluten-free brown sugar

¼ cup olive oil

¼ cup onions, finely chopped

1/3 cup lemon juice

Combine all ingredients together in a medium bowl. Marinade in the refrigerator for 4 hours.

Grill or bake the chicken for 15 to 20 minutes or until fully cooked.

CHICKEN FETA CHEESE

2 boneless chicken breast, sliced in strips

4 tablespoons olive oil

2 teaspoons gluten-free fresh pepper sauce

½ teaspoon salt

1 red bell pepper, chopped

1 yellow bell pepper, chopped

1 small onion, finely chopped

1 cup crumbled feta cheese (Boar's Head) (gluten-free)

Heat all the ingredients except feta cheese together in a large skillet until chicken is fully cooked, about 15 to 20 minutes.

Add feta cheese. Heat for 3 minutes.

CHICKEN ALFREDO

1 pound boneless chicken breast

¼ teaspoon pepper

¼ teaspoon salt

1 tablespoon olive oil

½ teaspoon dried thyme leaves

1 bag frozen mixed vegetables

1 container gluten-free Alfredo pasta sauce

In a large skillet, heat chicken with all ingredients except Alfredo sauce until fully cooked, about 15 to 20 minutes.

Add alfredo pasta sauce and heat for 5 minutes.

SOUTHWESTERN CHICKEN AND HASH

2 cups chicken breast, diced and cooked

2 cups potatoes, diced and peeled

½ cup red bell pepper

½ teaspoon salt

½ teaspoon black pepper

½ teaspoon Spice Hunter seasoning (gluten-free)

1 egg white

1 tablespoon olive oil

6 tablespoons gluten-free salsa

Boil potatoes and peel and cut into small cubes.

Combine all ingredients except salsa together in a large bowl; blend well.

Heat oil in a large skillet over medium heat for 8 minutes.

Spoon salsa over chicken.

CHICKEN PARMESAN

5 boneless chicken breasts

2 eggs, slightly beaten

1 cup kinnikinnick crispy chicken coating mix (gluten-free)

2 tablespoons olive oil

1 jar pasta sauce

1 cup shredded mozzarella (Boar's Head) (gluten-free)

Preheat oven to 375. Dip chicken in eggs, then bread crumbs.

In a large skillet, heat oil over medium-high and brown chicken.

Bake uncovered for 25 minutes.

FRIED CHICKEN

2 cups kinnikinnick crispy chicken coating mix (gluten-free)

1 teaspoon salt

¼ teaspoon pepper

1 frying chicken, cut up or chicken pieces

8 cups oil

Combine chicken mix, salt, pepper in plastic bag. Shake to coat.

Heat oil in large frying skillet. Add chicken and deep fry for 15 to 20 minutes. Add extra oil when needed.

CHILI-RUBBED PORK TENDERLOIN

1 pound pork tenderloin

1 teaspoon oil

1 garlic clove, finely chopped

1/8 teaspoon ground pepper

1 teaspoon salt

1 ½ teaspoon Spice Hunter chili power (gluten-free)

Mix all ingredients together except pork in a large bowl. Brush pork with oil and press spice mixture on the sides of the pork.

Heat oven to 375 and cook pork for 40 minutes. Cut pork into slices.

BREADED PORK CHOPS

4 boneless pork loin chops, ½-inch thick

½ teaspoon salt

½ teaspoon pepper

3 cups kinnikinnick crispy chicken coating mix (gluten-free)

3 tablespoons olive oil

Mix salt, pepper, chicken mix in a large bowl. Dip pork into mix.

In a large skillet, add oil and fry for 5 to 8 minutes on each side until fully cooked.

BARBECUE PORK CHOPS

4 boneless pork loin chops, ½-inch thick

Sprinkle with Spice Hunter pork seasoning (gluten-free)

3 tablespoons olive oil

In a large skillet, add oil and brown pork. Heat for 6 to 8 minutes on each side until it's fully cooked.

Add gluten free barbecue sauce. Heat for 2 minutes and serve.

MUSTARD HAM STEAK

1 large ham streak

2 tablespoons gluten-free yellow mustard

2 medium green onions

1/3 cup gluten-free maple syrup

In a large skillet, cook ham until brown, about 4 minutes on each side.

Microwave mixture on high for 20 to 30 minutes or until hot.

Place ham on serving dish platter; pour mixture over ham.

STRIP STEAKS WITH MANGO SALSA

4 boneless beef New York strip steaks

¼ cup red bell pepper, finely chopped

2 teaspoon seeded jalapeno chilies, finely chopped

1 teaspoon grated ginger roots, finely chopped

¼ cup peaches

1 tablespoon lime juice

1 small mango, cut in small pieces

2 teaspoons Spice Hunter Caribbean jerk seasoning (gluten-free)

1 jar salsa (gluten free)

In medium bowl, mix pepper, chilies, and ginger root. Stir in peaches, lime juice, and mango.

Set oven to broil. Sprinkle both sides of beef with jerk seasoning. Place on rack in broiler pan. Broil for 8 minutes on each side. Serve with salsa.

BEEF TENDERLOIN AND MUSHROOM

4 beef tenderloin steaks (1 ½ inches thick)

½ teaspoon salt

½ teaspoon pepper

6 s cold butter

1 ½ cup mushrooms, sliced

2 cloves garlic, finely chopped

¾ cup white wine

In large skillet over medium heat, sprinkle beef steaks with salt and pepper. Cook beef in butter 10 to 15 minutes, turning once, until deep brown.

In medium skillet over medium heat, add 1 tablespoon of the remaining butter to skillet. Add mushrooms and garlic. Cook 3 to 4 minutes, stirring occasionally. Add wine. Cook 2 to 3 minutes longer.

Beat remaining butter, 1 tablespoon at a time, into sauce with wire whisk just until melted. Serve mushrooms and sauce over beef.

LEMON PEPPER STEAK

4 beef sirloin or rib eye steaks (1 inch thick)

½ teaspoon fresh garlic, finely chopped

¼ cup butter, melted

2 tablespoons fresh basil

2 teaspoons Spice Hunter lemon-pepper seasoning (gluten-free)

2 medium bell peppers, finely chopped

Heat garlic, peppers, butter, and basil in a small skillet over medium heat.

Coat steak with lemon pepper.

Grill or broil for 10 to 15 minutes on each side. Brush tops of steaks with butter mixture.

BEEF STIR FRY

2 pounds boneless beef sirloin, cut into thin strips

2 cups water

1 bag fresh stir-fry vegetables

½ cup Eden organic tamari soy sauce (gluten-free)

1 medium onion, chopped

1 box white rice (gluten free)

¼ cup olive oil

In a medium skillet, add 2 teaspoons olive oil. Brown beef until fully cooked.

In the same skillet, heat water to boiling. Add soy sauce and vegetables. Heat to boiling.

Serve over white rice (gluten-free).

BASIL SALMON AND VEGETABLES

¼ cup Imagine organic chicken broth (gluten-free)

1 teaspoon Spice Hunter lemon pepper seasoning (gluten freegluten-free)

½ teaspoon salt

2 tablespoons fresh basil leaves, chopped

1 ½ pounds salmon fillets (½-inch thick)

2 large red bell peppers, chopped

2 medium onions, chopped

2 tablespoons butter

1 medium zucchini, chopped

In a medium skillet, melt butter over medium heat. Add onions, bell peppers, and zucchini. Cook and stir 3 minutes until vegetables are tender.

In a medium skillet, melt butter. Add broth, fish with lemon pepper and basil.
Cook for 6 minutes on each side until the fish is done.

Lay vegetables out and place fish over the vegetables.

BAKED SALMON OR RED SNAPPER

¼ teaspoon salt

¼ teaspoon ground cumin

1 tablespoon lemon juice

¼ cup butter

1 tablespoon fresh cilantro, chopped

½ teaspoon grated lemon peel

1 ½ pound salmon or red snapper (1 inch thick)

Heat oven to 425.

In a small bowl, mix butter, cilantro, and lemon peel. Place fish in casserole dish. Pour butter mixture over fish. Bake for 20 minutes until fish flakes easily with fork.

DILL TUNA OR SWORDFISH

1 tablespoon butter

1 tablespoon olive oil

1 ½ pound tuna or swordfish (¾ inch thick)

1 teaspoon salt

1 teaspoon pepper

½ cup small red onion, sliced

¾ cup orange juice

1 tablespoon chopped fresh dill weed

1 tablespoon butter

1 teaspoon grated orange peel

In a large skillet, heat butter and the oil over medium heat. Sprinkle both sides of fish with pepper and salt. Cook fish 4 minutes on each side until tender.

Add remaining ingredients together in skillet. Heat for 2 minutes and serve.

LEMON GARLIC HALIBUT STREAKS

2 pounds halibut (¾ inch thick)

¼ cup chopped fresh parsley

1 tablespoon grated lemon peel

¼ cup lemon juice

1 tablespoon olive oil

¼ teaspoon salt

¼ teaspoon pepper

2 cloves garlic, finely chopped

In a medium bowl, add lemon juice, olive oil, garlic, salt and pepper, lemon peels, and parsley. Marinade for 1 hour in the refrigerator.

In a large skillet, add the fish with marinade and cook for 4 minutes on each side or until fish is tender.

ITALIAN SEA BASS OR MAHI-MAHI

¼ cup Italian bread crumbs (Gillian's) (gluten-free)

¼ cup chopped fresh parsley

2 teaspoon grated lemon peel

1 tablespoon butter

1 Lb sea bass or mahi-mahi

¼ teaspoon salt

1 tablespoon lemon juice

Heat oven to 425.

In a small bowl, mix bread crumbs, parsley, lemon peel and butter.

Dip fish into mixture. Add lemon juice over fish.

Bake for 15 to 20 minutes or until fish flakes easily with a fork.

FISH FLORENTINE

¼ cup Red Mill white rice flour (gluten-free)

1 pound tilapia fillets (½-inch thick)

½ teaspoon salt

1 teaspoon Spice Hunter lemon pepper seasoning (gluten-free)

¼ cup butter

1 bag fresh baby spinach

½ red pepper, chopped

¼ cup slivered almonds (toasted)

In a small bowl, add flour, salt, lemon pepper. Dip fish into mixture.

In a large skillet, heat butter over medium heat. Cook fish for 6 to 8 minutes on each side until brown and fish flakes easily with fork.

Add spinach and bell peppers to butter in skillet. Cook for 2 to 4 minutes.

Spoon spinach mixture over fish. Add almonds.

FLOUNDER HERB FILLETS

1 pound founder (½-inch thick)

2 eggs

1 ¼ cup Gillian's bread crumbs (gluten-free)

1 teaspoon grated lemon peel

1 teaspoon dried marjoram leaves

½ teaspoon salt

½ teaspoon pepper

¼ cup olive oil

In a large bowl, beat eggs. Add bread crumbs, lemon peel, marjoram, salt, and pepper. Dip fish in mixture.

In a large skillet, heat olive oil over medium heat. Cook fish for 4 minutes on each side until browned and crisp and fish flakes easily with fork.

LEMON PEPPER SHRIMP

2 pounds fresh large shrimp

¼ cup butter

4 teaspoons Spice Hunter lemon pepper seasoning

In a large skillet, melt butter and add lemon pepper. Add shrimp. Cook over medium heat for 10 minutes.

SHRIMP RICE SKILLET

1 tablespoon olive oil

1 medium onion, chopped

¼ cup Imagine organic chicken broth (gluten-free)

1 cup cooked gluten-free white rice

1 cup sliced carrots

½ cup water

½ teaspoon Spice Hunter garlic pepper

2 cups fresh baby spinach

2 pound fresh shrimp (no tails)

¼ cup shredded parmesan cheese (Boar's Head) (gluten-free)

In a large skillet, heat oil over medium heat. Cook onions and shrimp for about 5 minutes.

Stir in carrots, water, rice, and garlic-pepper. Add spinach. Cover; simmer for 8 minutes.

FINAL NOTE

Make sure you use gluten-free ingredients. Read all labels. If you are uncertain, call the phone number on the label to verify ingredients. I have listed a whole list of gluten-free items in this book. Use them. If they are not in your store, call the manufactures and they will send them to you. Enjoy these recipes.

Made in the USA
Lexington, KY
03 February 2012